HOW TO PLAY

Here are some of the features of this special quiz book:

• Great way to start a conversation: Get to know new people and reacquaint yourself with old friends and family members at get-togethers

• A fun pastime: Discover an exciting way to pass your idle time and get rid of boredom without screens

• Turn-based: Take turns to ask " This or That" questions that your partner will answer without thinking too hard

• Series of Questions: You can make a rule for how many questions you can ask on each turn, usually one to five.

WOULD YOU RATHER...

THIS OR THIS?

THIS OR THAT...?
(MAKE YOUR CHOICE / EXPLAIN ANSWERS)

FROZEN VEGGIES OR CANNED?

SPIRAL OR STRAIGHT STAIRS?

COUNTRY SINGER OR
PROFESSIONAL ATHLETE?

WEAR SOMETHING BLUE OR
SOMETHING PINK?

ROSES OR SUNFLOWERS?

THIS OR THAT...?
(MAKE YOUR CHOICE / EXPLAIN ANSWERS)

PUMPKIN PIE OR APPLE PIE?

XBOX OR PLAYSTATION?

RUNNING OR WALKING?

FIREMAN OR POLICEMAN?

LONG OR SHORT HAIR?

THIS OR THAT...?
(MAKE YOUR CHOICE / EXPLAIN ANSWERS)

CAKE OR DONUTS?

FORD OR DODGE?

LAKE OR RIVER?

MARVEL OR DC COMICS?

MICKEY MOUSE OR
DORA THE EXPLORER?

THIS OR THAT...?
(MAKE YOUR CHOICE / EXPLAIN ANSWERS)

GREEN BEANS OR BROCCOLI?

CARNIVAL OR CIRCUS?

METAL OR WOOD?

CATCHER OR PITCHER?

BATMAN OR SUPERMAN?

THIS OR THAT...?
(MAKE YOUR CHOICE / EXPLAIN ANSWERS)

APPLES OR BANANAS?

TELEVISION OR A BOOK?

HUNTING OR FISHING?

WINTER OR SUMMER?

LAWYER OR CARPENTER?

This or That...?

Bacon or sausage?

Jeans and tee or a suit?

Football or baseball?

Rock star or race car driver?

Movies at home or in theaters?

THIS OR THAT...?
(MAKE YOUR CHOICE / EXPLAIN ANSWERS)

CHIPS WITH DIP OR
VEGETABLES AND DIP?

DANCING OR COOKING CLASSES?

WORKING IN A STORE OR
WORKING IN RESEARCH?

BRAINS OR BEAUTY?

HOME PETS: GIRAFFE OR HIPPO?

THIS OR THAT...?

(MAKE YOUR CHOICE / EXPLAIN ANSWERS)

HOT PRETZELS OR NACHOS?

THANKSGIVING OR EASTER?

CARDS OR BOARD GAMES?

SKATEBOARDING OR SWIMMING?

A JOB YOU LOVE OR
ONE THAT PAYS YOU MORE MONEY?

THIS OR THAT...?
(MAKE YOUR CHOICE / EXPLAIN ANSWERS)

BURGERS OR SEAFOOD?

FERRARI OR JAGUAR?

BOWLING OR TENNIS?

THUNDERSTORM OR SNOWSTORM?

PEN OR PENCIL?

THIS OR THAT...?

(MAKE YOUR CHOICE / EXPLAIN ANSWERS)

RIBS OR WINGS?

BOUND BOOK OR EBOOK?

ELEGANT OR CASUAL INTERIOR?

STRATEGY OR PUZZLE?

DRIVE OR FLY?

THIS OR THAT...?
(MAKE YOUR CHOICE / EXPLAIN ANSWERS)

CORN MUFFIN OR BLUEBERRY?

DETECTIVE NOVELS OR
SUPERHEROES?

ICE HOCKEY OR BASKETBALL?

SPRING OR FALL?

NEW YORK CITY OR VEGAS?

THIS OR THAT...?
(MAKE YOUR CHOICE / EXPLAIN ANSWERS)

TURKEY AND CHEESE OR
ROAST BEEF SUB?

AFRICA OR ASIA?

RUGS OR HARDWOOD FLOORS?

A PERSONAL TRAINER OR
WORK OUT ALONE?

ACTOR OR SUPERMODEL?

THIS OR THAT...?

(MAKE YOUR CHOICE / EXPLAIN ANSWERS)

COLD CEREAL OR OATMEAL?

BLUE OR RED?

WATCH SPORTS OR PLAY?

PUBLIC LIBRARY OR
BOOKSTORE?

SWIMMING POOL OR LAKE?

THIS OR THAT...?

(MAKE YOUR CHOICE / EXPLAIN ANSWERS)

SOUR CREAM AND ONION CHIPS
OR BARBECUE?

NEWSPAPER OR
ONLINE NEWS BLOG?

SPIDERMAN OR THE HULK?

LIVE IN THE DESERT OR
IN THE JUNGLE?

PILOT OR SHIP CAPTAIN?

THIS OR THAT...?

(MAKE YOUR CHOICE / EXPLAIN ANSWERS)

COFFEE OR TEA?

HORROR STORIES OR
MYSTERIES?

MEDICAL EXAMINER OR
EMERGENCY DOCTOR?

CHANDELIER OR LAMPS?

SHOWER OR BATH?

THIS OR THAT...?
(MAKE YOUR CHOICE / EXPLAIN ANSWERS)

SWEET POTATO OR
FRENCH FRIES?

BE CREATIVE OR GENIUS?

NIGHT OWL OR EARLY RISER?

BRUCE WILLIS OR
HARRISON FORD?

PACMAN OR TETRIS?

THIS OR THAT...?
(MAKE YOUR CHOICE / EXPLAIN ANSWERS)

CHEESEBURGER OR CALAMARI?

SWEATER OR HOODIE?

COMPUTER OR
GAME CONSOLES?

SILVER OR GOLD?

WORK ON A TEAM OR
TO WORK ALONE?

THIS OR THAT...?

(MAKE YOUR CHOICE / EXPLAIN ANSWERS)

CORN CHIPS OR DORITOS?

ANTHROPOLOGIST OR ASTRONOMER?

COSTUME PARTY OR POOL PARTY?

LIVE IN THE PAST OR PRESENT?

LOSE YOUR SENSE OF SMELL OR YOUR SENSE OF TASTE?

THIS OR THAT...?
(MAKE YOUR CHOICE / EXPLAIN ANSWERS)

BREAKFAST PIZZA OR
BREAKFAST SANDWICH?

GARDENING OR WALKING?

FLIP FLOPS OR WATER SHOES?

BE POPULAR AT SCHOOL OR
DATE SOMEONE POPULAR?

APARTMENT OR HOME?

THIS OR THAT...?

(MAKE YOUR CHOICE / EXPLAIN ANSWERS)

JUICE OR WATER?

BE GOOD AT MATH OR
BE AN AMAZING WRITER?

ROCK OR COUNTRY?

POLO OR HORSE RACING?

BUBBLE BATH OR
JUST A HOT SOAK?

THIS OR THAT...?
(MAKE YOUR CHOICE / EXPLAIN ANSWERS)

BAKED POTATO OR ONION RINGS?

AUDI OR BMW?

MANY CASUAL FRIENDS OR
JUST A FEW CLOSE FRIENDS?

GUITAR OR PIANO?

BE ABDUCTED BY
ZOMBIES OR ALIENS?

THIS OR THAT...?
(MAKE YOUR CHOICE / EXPLAIN ANSWERS)

ORANGES OR PEACHES?

CHANGE YOUR EYE COLOR OR
YOUR HAIR COLOR?

GAS OR CHARCOAL GRILL?

HUNTING TRIP OR SKI RESORT?

BE A SUPERHERO OR A WIZARD?

THIS OR THAT...?
(MAKE YOUR CHOICE / EXPLAIN ANSWERS)

TOOTSIE ROLLS OR SKITTLES?

BLONDE OR REDHEAD?

GRAND CANYON OR
JELLYSTONE?

COOK OR WAITRESS?

FACEBOOK OR TWITTER?

THIS OR THAT...?
(MAKE YOUR CHOICE / EXPLAIN ANSWERS)

SUGAR OR CHOCOLATE CHIP COOKIES?

TAKE A REST AT THE BEACH OR IN THE FOREST?

COUNTRY OR CITY?

COMPUTER OR GAME CONSOLES?

SECRETARY OR OFFICE MANAGER?

THIS OR THAT...?

GRAPE OR ORANGE?

BE ABLE TO FREEZE TIME OR
TRAVEL IN TIME?

CONTACTS OR GLASSES?

PROFESSIONAL BOWLER OR
POKER PLAYER?

KISSES OR HUGS?

THIS OR THAT...?
(MAKE YOUR CHOICE / EXPLAIN ANSWERS)

PRINGLES OR LAY'S?

COLLEGE OR TRADE SCHOOL?

KIDS OR PETS?

BE ABLE TO SPEAK TO ANIMALS
OR ON EVERY LANGUAGE
IN THE WORLD?

HEALTHY OR COMFORT FOOD?

THIS OR THAT...?

(MAKE YOUR CHOICE / EXPLAIN ANSWERS)

TACO BELL OR MCDONALD'S?

HAVE A LOT OF MONEY OR
BE GOOD LOOKING?

GHOST TOUR OR
HISTORICAL TOUR?

WRESTLER OR FOOTBALL PLAYER?

SPONGEBOB OR PATRICK?

THIS OR THAT...?
(MAKE YOUR CHOICE / EXPLAIN ANSWERS)

FAMILY-RUN OR CHAIN RESTAURANT?

SECURITY SYSTEM OR A DOG?

COMPUTER PROGRAMMER OR CRIMINOLOGIST (CSI)?

STAY AT YOUR CURRENT AGE OR BE 5 YEARS YOUNGER?

RICHES OR HAPPINESS?

THIS OR THAT...?
(MAKE YOUR CHOICE / EXPLAIN ANSWERS)

SWEETENED TEA OR
UNSWEETENED?

CAR OR PLANE?

MOOSE OR HEDGEHOG?

SELF-EMPLOYED OR
A COMPANY MAN?

ZOO OR AQUARIUM?

THIS OR THAT...?

(MAKE YOUR CHOICE / EXPLAIN ANSWERS)

ICE CREAM OR MILKSHAKE?

DOG OR CAT?

BE ABLE ONLY TO WHISPER OR
ONLY BE ABLE TO SHOUT?

TATTOO OR PIERCINGS?

MEETINGS ALL DAY OR
PRODUCING GOODS?

THIS OR THAT...?
(MAKE YOUR CHOICE / EXPLAIN ANSWERS)

BREAKFAST OR NO BREAKFAST?

COMEDY OR THRILLERS?

BLACK AND WHITE OR COLOR?

DEER OR BEAR?

AMERICA'S GOT TALENT OR AMERICAN IDOL?

THIS OR THAT...?

(MAKE YOUR CHOICE / EXPLAIN ANSWERS)

CHINESE OR JAPANESE FOOD?

ASK SILLY QUESTIONS OR
ANSWER THEM?

MOTORCYCLE OR BICYCLE?

DYED HAIR OR
NATURAL COLORS?

JOURNALIST OR PHOTOGRAPHER?

THIS OR THAT...?
(MAKE YOUR CHOICE / EXPLAIN ANSWERS)

RICE KRISPIES OR
CORN FLAKES?

TV SHOWS OR MOVIES?

VISIT SOMEBODY OR
TAKE GUESTS AT HOME?

NINJAS OR PIRATES?

TOUCH OR TASTE?

THIS OR THAT...?
(MAKE YOUR CHOICE / EXPLAIN ANSWERS)

JUICE OR SODA?

CREDIT CARD OR CASH?

BIG PARTY OR
SMALL GATHERING?

REALITY OR FICTION?

FASHION DESIGNER OR
INTERIOR DESIGNER?

THIS OR THAT...?

(MAKE YOUR CHOICE / EXPLAIN ANSWERS)

DARK CHOCOLATE OR WHITE CHOCOLATE?

NEW YORK OR LONDON?

LATE NIGHT OR EARLY MORNING?

FRIDAYS OR SATURDAYS?

NEWS ANCHOR OR METEOROLOGIST?

THIS OR THAT...?
(MAKE YOUR CHOICE / EXPLAIN ANSWERS)

SALT OR PEPPER?

ONLINE SHOPPING OR
IN-STORE SHOPPING?

PUPPIES OR KITTENS?

TEACHER OR ADMINISTRATOR?

SUNRISE OR SUNSET?

THIS OR THAT...?
(MAKE YOUR CHOICE / EXPLAIN ANSWERS)

POPCORN OR PEANUTS?

DISNEY CHANNEL OR
NICKELODEON?

SUN OR MOON?

BEARD OR CLEAN-SHAVEN?

AUTHOR OR
ADVERTISING AGENT?

THIS OR THAT...?
(MAKE YOUR CHOICE / EXPLAIN ANSWERS)

PEANUTS OR ALMONDS?

FISH OR BIRDS?

HORROR MOVIE OR
COMEDY MOVIE?

POST INSTAGRAM PICTURES
OF FOOD OR YOURSELF?

LAWYER OR DOCTOR?

THIS OR THAT...?

(MAKE YOUR CHOICE / EXPLAIN ANSWERS)

MEAT OR FISH?

MOUNTAINS OR THE OCEAN?

OFFICE WORK OR OUTSIDE WORK?

A 99% CHANCE TO WIN $100,000 OR A 50-50 CHANCE AT $10 MILLION?

PASSENGER OR DRIVER?

THIS OR THAT...?

(MAKE YOUR CHOICE / EXPLAIN ANSWERS)

NO FOOD OR NO SLEEP?

BE LUCKY OR TALENTED?

TELEPORTATION OR TIME TRAVEL?

LIVE IN HAWAII OR ALASKA?

FBI AGENT OR SHERIFF?

THIS OR THAT...?

(MAKE YOUR CHOICE / EXPLAIN ANSWERS)

HUNGRY OR THIRSTY?

THE PERFECT JOB OR
THE PERFECT RELATIONSHIP?

BE STRONG OR SMART?

VISIT BARCELONA OR PARIS?

WORK FOR APPLE OR GOOGLE?

THIS OR THAT...?

(MAKE YOUR CHOICE / EXPLAIN ANSWERS)

BAGELS OR ENGLISH MUFFINS?

BE RICH OR FAMOUS?

LIVE AS YOURSELF OR
LIVE AS SOMEONE ELSE?

SNOW OR RAIN?

SECRET SERVICE OR
PRIVATE BODYGUARD?

THIS OR THAT...?
(MAKE YOUR CHOICE / EXPLAIN ANSWERS)

SMOOTHIE OR ICE CREAM?

DINNER DATE OR MOVIE DATE?

MEET BARACK OBAMA OR
DONALD TRUMP?

SHORTS OR SKIRTS?

FISHERMAN OR LUMBERJACK?

THIS OR THAT...?
(MAKE YOUR CHOICE / EXPLAIN ANSWERS)

CRAB OR LOBSTER?

WASHING THE DISHES OR
MOWING THE LAWN?

BE STUCK AT AGE 8 OR 80?

READ FOR TWO HOURS OR
WRITE FOR TWO HOURS?

SPEAK GERMAN OR FRENCH?

THIS OR THAT...?
(MAKE YOUR CHOICE / EXPLAIN ANSWERS)

BROCCOLI OR CARROT?

LIVE IN 1968 OR IN 2068?

SHOWER GEL OR SOAP?

BE A DRAGON OR UNICORN?

CAPTAIN AMERICA OR
IRON MAN?

THIS OR THAT...?

STEAK OR BURGER?

A SMALL FAMILY OR
A LARGE FAMILY?

VISIT IRAN OR PAKISTAN?

BE FAMOUS ONLINE OR
IN REAL LIFE?

WORK ON TESLA OR SPACEX?

THIS OR THAT...?
(MAKE YOUR CHOICE / EXPLAIN ANSWERS)

CRACKERS OR
SESAME SEED BAGELS?

SUN OR MOON?

MORNING OR EVENING?

KNOW THE ENDING OF EVERY
NEW MOVIE BEFORE YOU WATCHING
OR WATCHING ONLY OLD MOVIES?

WONDER WOMAN OR SUPERGIRL?

THIS OR THAT...?
(MAKE YOUR CHOICE / EXPLAIN ANSWERS)

RED OR GREEN APPLES?

TRAVEL THE WORLD OR FOCUS ON YOUR CAREER?

SLEEP WITH CLOTHES OR NAKED?

NEW PHONE OR A NEW LAPTOP?

ROLLER SKATING OR ICE SKATING?

THIS OR THAT...?
(MAKE YOUR CHOICE / EXPLAIN ANSWERS)

VANILLA OR CHOCOLATE?

LIVE IN SAN FRANCISCO OR MIAMI?

SLEEP ON THE LEFT OR THE RIGHT SIDE OF THE BED?

MORE MONEY OR MORE TIME?

ROLLER COASTERS OR BUMPER CARS?

THIS OR THAT....?
(MAKE YOUR CHOICE / EXPLAIN ANSWERS)

EGGS OR BAGELS?

TOYOTA OR HONDA?

MEET MARK ZUCKERBERG OR
ELON MUSK?

TEXTING OR PHONE CALLS?

SNOWBALL FIGHT OR
WATER BALLOON FIGHT?

THIS OR THAT...?
(MAKE YOUR CHOICE / EXPLAIN ANSWERS)

GUMMY WORMS OR
GUMMY BEARS?

RADIO OR TELEVISION?

PONYTAIL OR PIGTAILS?

GIVING A GIFT OR
RECEIVING A GIFT?

GIVE UP LOVE OR SUCCESS?

THIS OR THAT...?

(MAKE YOUR CHOICE / EXPLAIN ANSWERS)

ICED TEA OR HOT TEA?

GLOVES OR MITTENS?

MARKERS OR CRAYONS?

BUNNY OR SQUIRREL?

HALLOWEEN OR
YOUR BIRTHDAY?

THIS OR THAT...?

(MAKE YOUR CHOICE / EXPLAIN ANSWERS)

WHITE MEAT OR DARK MEAT?

ROSES OR TULIPS?

JUSTIN TIMBERLAKE OR
JUSTIN BIEBER?

WORK OR SCHOOL?

AUTHOR OR EDITOR?

THIS OR THAT...?
(MAKE YOUR CHOICE / EXPLAIN ANSWERS)

PASTA OR RICE?

BIG EARS OR BIG NOSE?

CANOEING OR KAYAKING?

GRAMMYS OR OSCARS?

COWBOYS OR ALIENS?

THIS OR THAT...?
(MAKE YOUR CHOICE / EXPLAIN ANSWERS)

CHOCOLATE OR HARD CANDY?

DUST OR VACUUM?

MAKEUP OR NO MAKEUP?

TIE OR NO TIE?

SISTER OR BROTHER?

THIS OR THAT...?
(MAKE YOUR CHOICE / EXPLAIN ANSWERS)

PICKLES OR CUCUMBERS?

PERSONAL CHEF OR
PERSONAL FITNESS TRAINER?

SNAKE OR LIZARD?

PERFECT TEETH OR
PERFECT HAIR?

NOISE OR SILENCE?

THIS OR THAT...?

(MAKE YOUR CHOICE / EXPLAIN ANSWERS)

KETCHUP OR MUSTARD?

MINIMUM OR MAXIMUM?

HEART OR SOUL?

ARMED OR UNARMED?

PARTY PLANNER OR
WEDDING ASSIST?

THIS OR THAT...?

(MAKE YOUR CHOICE / EXPLAIN ANSWERS)

CRUSHED ICE OR CUBED ICE?

TALK BEFORE THINKING OR
THINK BEFORE TALKING?

EMAIL OR LETTER?

ADVENTUROUS OR CAUTIOUS?

BOXERS OR BRIEFS?

THIS OR THAT...?
(MAKE YOUR CHOICE / EXPLAIN ANSWERS)

HONEY MUSTARD OR
BBQ SAUCE?

NEUTRAL OR BRIGHT COLORS?

JUPITER OR SATURN?

OUTGOING OR SHY?

DAY OR NIGHT?

THIS OR THAT...?
(MAKE YOUR CHOICE / EXPLAIN ANSWERS)

EXPRESSO OR LATTE?

MATCHING OR
MISMATCHED SOCKS?

EYES OR SMILE?

SELFIES OR GROUP PHOTOS?

DESKTOP OR LAPTOP?

THIS OR THAT...?

(MAKE YOUR CHOICE / EXPLAIN ANSWERS)

THAI FOOD OR INDIAN FOOD?

BACKPACKING AROUND EUROPE
OR SOUTH EAST ASIA?

SITTING OR STANDING?

BEING TOO WARM OR
TOO COLD?

THE FLINTSTONES OR
THE SIMPSONS?

THIS OR THAT...?

(MAKE YOUR CHOICE / EXPLAIN ANSWERS)

TOAST OR EGGS?

HAT OR SUNGLASSES?

WILD ANIMALS OR
DOMESTIC ANIMALS?

DRUMS OR GUITARS?

FLY AN AIRPLANE OR
DRIVE A FIRE TRUCK?

THIS OR THAT...?

(MAKE YOUR CHOICE / EXPLAIN ANSWERS)

MILK OR JUICE?

BE A CYBORG OR A ROBOT?

CHECKERS OR CHESS?

ANTIQUE OR BRAND NEW?

GAS STATION ATTENDANT OR
SALES MANAGER?

THIS OR THAT...?
(MAKE YOUR CHOICE / EXPLAIN ANSWERS)

LOW CALORIE OR
TASTES GREAT?

STUDENT OR TEACHER?

PERFUME OR BODY SPRAY?

UNDERSTAND ANY LANGUAGE
OR BE ABLE TO PLAY
ANY INSTRUMENT?

ANIMATOR OR BABYSITTER?

THIS OR THAT...?
(MAKE YOUR CHOICE / EXPLAIN ANSWERS)

COCONUT MILK OR
FROZEN YOGURT?

STOP OR GO?

NUMBERS OR LETTERS?

NETFLIX OR YOUTUBE?

ELECTRICIAN OR ENGINEER?

THIS OR THAT....?

(MAKE YOUR CHOICE / EXPLAIN ANSWERS)

HOTCAKE OR WAFFLE?

HAVE A PURPLE NOSE OR GREEN EARS?

NEW CLOTHES OR NEW PHONE?

LIVE IN THE SKY OR UNDER THE SEA?

WIN AN OLYMPIC GOLD MEDAL OR OSCAR AWARD?

THIS OR THAT...?

DIET SODA OR
REGULAR SODA?

TRASH OR TREASURE?

A COWBOY HAT OR KNIT CAP?

MANICURE OR PEDICURE?

FLY A KITE OR
RIDE ON A SCOOTER?

THIS OR THAT...?
(MAKE YOUR CHOICE / EXPLAIN ANSWERS)

DRINK HOT CHOCOLATE OR
CHOCOLATE MILK?

TAN OR PALE?

JINGLE BELLS OR
LET IT SNOW?

PLAY GAMES ON A PHONE OR
PLAY A BOARD GAME?

BE BALD OR HAVE LONG HAIR?

THIS OR THAT...?
(MAKE YOUR CHOICE / EXPLAIN ANSWERS)

PUDDING OR CUSTARD?

BE POOR AND ATTRACTIVE
OR RICH AND UGLY?

JOKES OR RIDDLES?

SKY DIVING OR
BUNGEE JUMPING?

CREATE A NEW GAME OR
WRITE A SONG?

THIS OR THAT...?
(MAKE YOUR CHOICE / EXPLAIN ANSWERS)

DESSERT OR FRUIT?

INVISIBLE OR INVINCIBLE?

YES OR NO?

WITCHES OR WIZARDS?

THIS OR THAT?

THIS OR THAT...?
(WRITE YOUR QUESTIONS)

THIS OR THAT...?
(WRITE YOUR QUESTIONS)

THIS OR THAT...?
(WRITE YOUR QUESTIONS)

PLEASE, LEAVE A REVIEW.

IF YOU HAVE ENJOYED THIS BOOK,
PLEASE CONSIDER LEAVING A SHORT REVIEW
ON THE BOOKS AMAZON PAGE.
IT WILL HELP OTHERS TO MAKE AN INFORMED
DECISION BEFORE BUYING MY BOOK.

THANK YOU SO MUCH.

REGARDS,
CHARLIE

Made in the USA
Middletown, DE
23 March 2020